AMERICAN INDIAN
TRADITIONS AND CEREMONIES

AMERICAN INDIAN
TRADITIONS AND CEREMONIES

KAREN BERMAN

JG
PRESS

Published in the USA 1997 by JG Press
Distributed by World Publications, Inc.

The JG Press imprint is a trademark
of JG Press, Inc.
455 Somerset Avenue
North Dighton, MA 02764

Produced by
Brompton Books Corporation
15 Sherwood Place
Greenwich, CT 06830
USA

Copyright © 1997
Brompton Books Corporation

ISBN 1-57215-238-9

Printed in China

PAGE 1: A Kwakiutl Sun
Mask made of carved and
painted wood and painted
cloth, c. 1880.

PAGE 2: Navajo textile —
Teec Nos Pos Style, weaving
by Marian Nez, c. 1993.

PAGE 3: This bowl by
renowned San Ildefonso potter
Maria Martinez was placed
in a kiva to hold corn for the
next year's planting.

THIS PAGE: A Piegan travois.
The horse travois enabled
the nomadic Plains tribes to
mobilize quickly in pursuit of
the bison.

This book is dedicated to the memory of my parents,

Abe and Janice Berman, whose love colors everything I do.

CONTENTS

INTRODUCTION

When we look back at peoples who have fallen victim to genocide, it is their suffering that we remember, and not the flowering of culture that came before their tears. In the eyes of history, the renaissance of Eastern European Jewry is often overshadowed by the horror of the Holocaust; the charms of Armenian life pale beside the devastation they suffered at the hands of the Ottomans; the traditions of black South Africans remain vague to outsiders who witnessed the brutality of apartheid on the evening news.

The same is true of North American Indians; we remember their trials — Wounded Knee and the Trail of Tears and countless unnamed losses — but many of us know little about the peoples who occupied North America for thousands of years before Europe dared to imagine the New World.

That's a shame, for while it's important to remember the tragedy of genocide lest we allow history to repeat itself, it is just as important not to define its victims solely by their suffering, but to see them in all the complexity of their best days. We marvel at the North American Indians, at the ingenuity of the igloo, the precision of porcupine-quill embroidery, the economy of the arrowhead, the beauty of a patterned basket, and we are enriched and inspired.

North American Indian culture was, to paraphrase Walt Whitman, vast; it contained multi-

LEFT: Varied though the North American tribal cultures were, they shared a respect for nature and for the earth's resources. Some saw nature as a fearsome force to be appeased by means of offerings and ceremonies; others believed the spirits present in nature were benevolent "brothers" to humanity. Here, a bustling encampment at Glacier National Park in Montana, circa 1926, affords access to both land and water.

ABOVE: A 19th century village of the Kwakiutl, a Northwest Coast tribe. Abundant forests and plentiful supplies of salmon and other marine life gave rise to traditions both practical and cultural; Northwest Coast peoples lived in sturdy wooden structures, fished from wooden boats and decorated their homes with elaborately carved wooden totems.

RIGHT: Although there were hundreds of North American Indian tongues, written language was not widespread, so oral traditions took on greater importance. Here, an Apache storytelling group is captured on film by Edward S. Curtis, who devoted his life to photographing the North American Indians.

FAR RIGHT: Some tribes chronicled their lives by painting or carving stone. "Newspaper Rock," at Newspaper Rock State Park in Utah, is a good example of prehistoric North American Indian pictograph illustration.

tudes. At its height between 1000 B.C. and A.D. 1000 it was comprised of some 600 different tribal societies who spoke almost as many languages and lived according to a variety of political, social and religious designs. In most of these tribes (as in most other societies the world over), important occasions, communal hopes and aspirations and individual rites of passage were marked by ceremony, while the business of daily living was colored by tradition. The beginning of buffalo hunting season, the hope for enough rainfall to produce a plentiful harvest, a youngster's passage into puberty — each offered ample reason for a ceremony. Likewise, the way a Pueblo woman wore her blanket over her left shoulder, never her right (only the dead reversed directions); the way the Haida positioned their houses side by side to face the sea; the way a Cheyenne infant's umbilical cord was placed in a pouch attached to his cradleboard for good luck, was all a matter of tradition.

These traditions and ceremonies evolved over time; just how they did, no one knows for sure, because North American Indian cultures were largely oral, not written, and many of them encouraged their tribal storytellers' personal interpretations of communal lore. What we do know is based on archaeological evidence, as well as the written words and pictures of the early European explorers and settlers, and the reminiscences and practices of the surviving North American tribes.

The combined resources of geology and archaeology indicate that the North American Indians originally came from Asia. Estimates vary, but sometime between 40,000 and 10,000 years ago, the vast glaciers of the Ice Age froze large expanses of sea water and uncovered the land that is now beneath the Bering Sea. Called Beringia or the Bering Land Bridge, this land mass connected what is now Siberia and Alaska, and legions of prehistoric peoples crossed over it on foot. Gradually — over centuries — they made their way through what is now North America. Early on, much of the northern part of the continent was enveloped in glacier, but a narrow strip of land along the Rockies was exposed, and that, say the scientists, became the immigrants' pathway. Slowly, they made their way south, and as the glaciers receded, east and west. Some settled down and formed communities, while others continued on until they had reached the southern tip of what is now South America. Slightly farther north, great societies emerged in Mesoamerica. The Aztecs, the Mayas and the Incas developed sophisticated systems of government, religion, architecture, agriculture, astronomy and in the case of the Mayas, a unique system of written hieroglyphics. Because of their technological advances, scholars often categorize theses societies separately from the peoples of the north.

In North America, the earliest human inhabitants were nomadic big game hunters. Known to archaeologists as Paleo-Indians, they hunted mastodon, mammoth, giant sloth, several now-extinct species of huge bison, and other animals. Then, sometime between 10,000 and 8,000 B.C. the Ice Age ended and the warmer climate of the continent doomed these big game animals to extinction. The Paleo-Indians adapted to the

BELOW: Entire civilizations lived and died before the Europeans ever set foot in the New World. The Mound Builders, who constructed earthen burial mounds, were skilled carvers. This marine shell miniature mask was found at a Southeastern Mound Culture site and dates from A.D. 1300-1500.

~~~~~~~~~~~~~~~~~~~

ABOVE: This Pre-Columbian pottery jar, found in Arkansas, is incised with a feline effigy.

RIGHT: Early Southwestern peoples built structures of adobe and stone, often in canyons or near riverbeds. Around A.D. 1,000, climatic changes forced them to relocate to mountain cliffs. This photo shows the ruins of the White House, an Anasazi sandstone dwelling in Arizona's Canyon de Chelly.

change by turning to other sources of food: smaller game, fish, nuts, seeds, roots and berries. Archaeologists call this era, which began around 7,000 B.C., the Archaic Period. The need for new sources of food reverberated throughout North American Indian life. New food sources required new tools, such as the mortar and pestle and the *mano* and *metate* (a hand-held stone and flat slab) for crushing seeds and nuts, baskets for gathering berries and plants, pottery for storage, and hooks and spears for fishing. The peoples of the East and Southwest turned to agriculture, and that development brought even more change. Some of these tribes gave up their wandering lifestyles entirely and settled into permanent villages. Others adopted semi-permanent encampments during the growing season. These villages and encampments gradually became larger, as farms fed more and more people. And because crops required regular tending, daily life took on an order that the mercurial lifestyle of hunting had never provided. Weather took on a renewed importance to these farmers, as well.

Several of these early farming societies were born, prospered and faded away well before the arrival of the Europeans. The Mound Builders, so called because they constructed earthen mounds as burial sites, flourished in the Ohio River Valley area from about 500 B.C. to A.D. 400 and in the Mississippi River Valley and surrounding river valleys from about A.D. 700 through the 16th century. The Ohio societies, first the Adena and then the Hopewell cultures (named for the present-day towns where their artifacts were found) combined hunting and gathering with agriculture. These peoples were able to rally enough community support to build burial mounds that were thousands of feet long. They carved elaborate designs onto their tools and burial objects, and must have engaged in trade with nomadic cultures, as some of their carvings are of materials, such as obsidian, that are not native to their region. The Adena and Hopewell cultures were gradually absorbed into the Mississippi culture, which covered the Tennessee, Cumberland and part of the Ohio river valleys, as well as the Mississippi Valley. French explorers of the early 1700s who chanced to observe the last of the Mississippi tribes noted that the culture was socially stratified

Received from the honorable Thomas and Richard Penn Esq.rs true and absolute Proprietaries of Pennsylvania by the hands of the honorable Sir William Johnson Baronet the Sum of ten thousand Dollars being the full consideration of the Lands lately sold to them by the Indians of the six Nations at the late Treaty of Fort Stanwix We say received this Twenty Eighth day of July — Anno Domini 1769 — for ourselves and the other Indians of the six Nations and their confederates and dependant Tribes for whom we act and by whom we are appointed and empowered —

into priestly and commoner classes. They lived on flat-topped platform mounds that were designed for ceremonial use rather than as burial sites, and cultivated large-scale farms. The Mississippi culture was a complex one, but by the early 1700s it had all but disappeared; archaeologists believe epidemics wiped out almost the entire population.

Another society that had disappeared by the time the Europeans arrived was that of the Anasazi, the early Pueblo peoples. The Anasazi lived in what is now Arizona, New Mexico and Colorado, and built multi-story stone and adobe housing complexes that were typically divided into several hundred rooms. They farmed the hot, dry land by means of irrigation canals and developed an extensive trading network with the Mesoamerican cultures to the south. Archaeologists believe that droughts forced them to disperse and form new communities or join other tribes near the region's major rivers.

Meanwhile, as these early farming societies faded away, hundreds of other tribes — hunters and gatherers as well as farmers — emerged and thrived throughout North America, having successfully met the Archaic Era's challenge of finding new food sources. Geography and ecology determined what kinds of foods were available in different areas and what each tribe's primary identity would be. These fundamental adaptations in turn shaped other aspects of their lives. Whether a tribe was nomadic or sedentary, what kind of shelter its people lived in, even what they believed about the universe around them were all influenced by their continual quest for food. Those who relied primarily on hunting, according to Ake Hultkranz in *Native Religions of North America*, practiced animal ceremonialism, while those who depended on agriculture practiced fertility rites and rain ceremonies. Farming societies tended to believe that people originally came to this world from subterranean underworlds — the way plants do. Hunting and foraging tribes, on the other hand, told stories of a Great Spirit who created the world and gave gifts of land and resources to human beings, who

according to some tellings, made an epic trek, sometimes guided by a sacred pole or seashell, to get to that land.

Political organization, too, was often influenced by Archaic Indians' quest for subsistence. In the southern region of the Great Basin, the arid land offered the Indians a grudging diet of rodents, insects, lizards and roots. There, the Indians traveled in family groups small enough to subsist on these small-scale resources. At the other extreme were the Iroquois of the Northeast Woodlands, who developed a complex confederation of tribes with councils to settle feuds and territorial disputes peacefully. In between, there were many tribes whose chiefs were chosen for their charisma or their bravery in battle and the hunt; they had little power over the daily lives of their subjects. Still other tribes' social structures were defined by strict class hierarchies.

Based on their adaptations to regional climate and food supply, archaeologists have divided the Indians of North America into nine culture areas:

➤ The Arctic, comprising the northernmost coast of Alaska, Canada and all of Greenland, was home to the Inuit (called Eskimos, meaning "eaters of raw flesh," by the neighboring Algonquins) and the island-dwelling Aleuts.

➤ The Sub-Arctic, the desolate forest land that covers the northern interior of Canada and interior Alaska, was inhabited by the Athapascans (including the Hare, Chipewyans and Dogrib) to the west and the Algonquins (including the Cree and Ojibwa) to the east.

➤ The Northeast Woodlands, the forested area that now comprises southeastern Canada and the northeastern United States, was occupied by three major confederations: the Iroquois (including the Mohawks, Senecas, Oneidas, Onondagas and Cayugas), the Algonquin (including the Penobscot, Abnaki and Delaware) and the Siouan.

➤ The Southeast, which covered the region from the Gulf of Mexico and the Atlantic Ocean inland to the present-day states of Virginia and Kentucky, was home to the Cherokee, Tuscarora, Choctaw, Chickasaw and Creek tribes, and later a hybrid tribe of refugees, the Seminoles.

➤ The Great Plains and Prairies, which covered the present-day Midwest, was occupied by the Mandan, Sioux, Crow, Blackfeet, Comanche and Cheyenne tribes.

➤ The Southwest, the arid desert just north of Mexico, was inhabited by the Zuñi, Hopi and Pueblo tribes, as well as the equestrian Apache and Navajo.

ABOVE: Southwestern cultures
are renowned for their clay
pottery. The various tribes and
pueblo communities all worked
in distinctive styles that have
been passed from generation
to generation, some favoring
geometric patterns and others,
figurative designs. These prehistoric bowls are from Pueblo
Bonito in Chaco Canyon,
New Mexico.

- California, covering the present-day state, was inhabited by the Pomos, Yuroks, Hupas, Miwoks and Chumash.

- The Great Basin, the land between the Rockies and the Sierra Nevada mountains in present-day Nevada, Utah, Idaho, Oregon, Washington and British Columbia, is sometimes divided in two by archaeologists. The arid southern sector was home to the Shoshoni, Paiute, Ute and Bannock, while the lush northern sector, sometimes called the Plateau, was inhabited by the Spokane, Wenatche, Yakima, Walla Walla, Coeur D'Alene, Nez Percé and Flathead tribes.

- The Northwest Coast, the fertile coastal area covering present-day Washington, Oregon, Vancouver and coastal Alaska, was occupied by the Haida, Tlingit, Kwakiutl and Chinook tribes.

These culture areas supported societies that were vastly different from one another. Yet, distortions by early chroniclers and later by Hollywood, have led many of us today to mistakenly lump all Indians together in a single culture. Thanks to Hollywood, the most common image of the North American Indian is that of the brave in a feathered headdress mounted on horseback. This brave did exist, but only in the Great Plains region — ironically, the last part of the continent to be settled by Indian tribes. Because of its sparse vegetation, the region was largely unpopulated for hundreds of years; it was only after other areas became too crowded — and after European colonists forced their way onto Indian land in the east and elsewhere — that the Plains became a North American Indian homeland. The introduction of the horse by the Spanish conquistadors made the harsh Plains landscape much more navigable.

Likewise, North American Indians have been called primitive, but this is too simplistic a term for peoples who devised such complex responses to environmental imperatives ranging from the frozen tundra of Alaska to the steamy wetlands of Florida. True, for the most part they lacked the knowledge of metalworking that, as early as 1500 B.C., had transformed the lives of their counterparts in Europe and the Middle East. A few North American cultures did use copper and silver for jewelry and ornamentation, but most of the Indians of North America remained firmly in the Stone Age, making

BELOW: Drinking vessels from Pueblo Bonito bear characteristic geometric designs.

tools and other implements of stone, wood, bone, hide, and whatever else the land yielded to them, until the arrival of the Europeans in the 1500s. When the Europeans did introduce their metal tools and firearms, as well as their horses, beads and cloth, the North American Indians eagerly integrated them into their lives. In the case of the horse and the gun, European goods revolutionized North American Indian life; they streamlined the buffalo hunt, speeded up transportation, modernized warfare and created a new source of wealth. Sadly, even as they improved North American Indian life, these same innovations, more plentiful in the hands of the white invaders, proved to be the Indians' undoing — along with European diseases to which they had no immunity.

Despite their differences, the peoples of the various culture areas shared a common outlook: they believed that the supernatural forces at the source of life were present throughout nature, and that these forces demanded humanity's respect. This concept was understood in various ways by different peoples. Some tribes believed the spirit world could turn hostile if not continu- ally appeased with the proper ceremonies. Others stressed the idea that all living things were part of one family and that if humans took nourishment from members of that family, they were obliged to do so with proper respect. Common to most of these world views was the assumption that the land and its resources were a sacred gift entrusted to them, and they were obliged to defend that sacred trust.

When the Europeans first arrived in the New World in the 1500s, the native population is estimated to have been between eight and fifteen million. After a few hundred years of struggle with the invaders (who eventually included the new United States government) only a few hundred thousand North American Indians survived, and most were confined to reservations.

But these proud native cultures did not die. New generations, now numbering nearly two million in the United States and Canada, have looked to the past for spiritual guidance. They have listened to their elders and studied the work of the archaeologists, and revived the old ceremonies and traditions.

THE CYCLE OF LIFE

N orth American Indians' lives were governed by tradition and ceremony from the cradle-board to the grave. In this, they were not unlike cultures all over the world. In many tribes, puberty was the most important milestone in an individual's life, more important than marriage. But each major event — birth, puberty, marriage, death and countless occasions in between — was observed in a way that had meaning to the celebrants.

In most North American Indian tribes, the birth of a child was a happy event. The Cree, an Algonquin tribe of the Northeast Woodlands and the Sub-Arctic, examined the newborn carefully for birthmarks or other features that would provide a link to a deceased relative; if one was found, the child was named for that relative. Each child was also linked with an animal spirit who, like a member of the family, was obliged to help in times of trouble. On the Plains, the new-born's family often hired a warrior to give their child a name. In the Southwest, where corn was sacred, the most perfect cobs were reserved for newborn babies, who, like their elders, wore body paint; babies' body paint consisted of mother's milk and ochre. Southwestern infants also received doll-sized models of Kachinas, spirits who were central to the region's religious beliefs. Doting families of the Plains and Great Basin saved the new baby's umbilical cord and placed it in a decorated bag, which was often fashioned in the shape of a turtle or lizard. This bag was

LEFT: In many North American Indian tribes, cradleboards were used to carry infants. These were often elaborately decorated, as can be seen in this photo of an Apsaroke mother and child.

ABOVE RIGHT: This Pueblo cradleboard had a sturdy base of wood, which would be covered with swaddling and decorated, often with objects thought to bring good luck to the baby.

attached to the cradleboard or hung around the baby's neck in order to bring good luck and long life. Mothers of many North American Indian cultures carried their children swaddled in cradleboards on their backs for at least the baby's first year. Often, the child's head would be fixed to the cradleboard to flatten its skull, a trait that many tribes considered beautiful. In the cold of the Arctic, a sling in the mother's parka served as a baby carrier, and the baby nestled inside to benefit from the mother's warmth.

Not all babies were welcomed into the world; the harsher the environment, the more strain another life put on the community. In the Arctic, when food was scarce, female infanticide was practiced; male babies were considered more valuable to the community because they would eventually become hunters. Female infanticide was also practiced in the Sub-Arctic, sometimes by mothers wishing to spare their daughters a hard life. In arid southern parts of the Great Basin, infanticide was practiced on babies born with birth defects.

While birth was usually a joyous event, the woman's role in the beginnings of life was regarded with a mixture of suspicion and awe that gave rise to numerous customs. Chief among them was isolation during birth. Women of the Northeast Woodlands went alone to the woods

LEFT: An Osage girl wearing a robe decorated with appliqued ribbon. She was photographed at the Louisiana Purchase Exposition of 1904 in St. Louis, Missouri.

ABOVE: In the cold of the Arctic, Inuit mothers carried their babies in pouches inside their fur coats, so that the children could benefit from their mothers' body heat. This mother and child were photographed in 1915 in Nome, Alaska, by H.G. Kaiser.

BELOW: Decoration on cradleboards was intricate and expressive. On the left, an elaborately beaded Oglala Sioux carrier celebrates the U.S. flag; Chief Red Cloud, an Oglala Sioux hero; and General L. Smith. On the right, a Cheyenne carrier depicts animals in beadwork.

RIGHT: Children's clothing was often a reflection in miniature of adult attire. Here, the decorations on an Arapaho child's moccasins with leggings shows the results of this Plains tribe's skill at trading: mass-produced glass beads and tin cone ornaments.

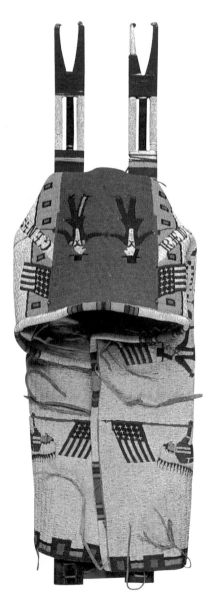

to give birth, and women of the Sub-Arctic also gave birth alone. Those of the Arctic bore their children alone in huts near their homes. These same huts were used during menstruation, when women were thought to be unclean and were kept away from the community. Isolation was not the rule throughout the continent, however; women of the Great Plains gave birth in teepees, attended by midwives. Nor were men excluded from birth rituals. In central California, it was the father who went into seclusion for four days after the birth of his child. Among the Great Basin peoples, a man was forbidden to twist any cord while his wife was pregnant, for fear that he would cause the baby to strangle in the womb.

This wary attitude toward women and birth carried over to another aspect of female biology: menses. A girl's first menstrual period was often cause for celebration, but subsequent periods were typically rewarded with isolation from the community. In the southern part of the Great Basin, girls were secluded for up to thirty days at their first menstrual period, while in the north, they could be isolated for longer. In the Southwest, girls were isolated for four days each month. Northwest Coast girls of the Nootka tribe were also subject to isolation during their menstrual periods. In the Arctic, when a young girl had her first menstrual period, she went into isolation in the hut near her house; monthly isolations continued throughout her life. During their menstrual

ABOVE: In some tribes of the Plains and Prairies, a newborn's umbilical cord was preserved in a decorated bag that was attached to the cradleboard for good luck. This photo shows a Sioux umbilical amulet of beaded hide.

LEFT: This Comanche boy's fringed hide shirt dates from the mid-19th century.

periods, Arctic women were prohibited from touching their husbands' hunting gear or going near the river or the sea for fear of contamination.

Isolation during menses was by no means the only observance of passage into puberty. Coming of age was, in many tribes, the most important event in a person's life and it was marked by endurance tests and feted with feasts and ceremonies. Both girls and boys underwent these initiation rites, but they were treated quite differently.

Much of North American Indian spiritual life centered on the individual's relationship with the supernatural, often through dreams and visions. It is not surprising, then, that several tribes required a boy to seek a vision in order to become a man. Often, these Vision Quests were tied to tests of endurance. Southern California boys were given jimson weed to induce stupor and encourage visions. Once a boy had received his vision, he painted his body and came before his elders for a ceremony in which he had to lie in an open grave and jump out, to symbolize rebirth after death. Then, he would climb into a pit full of biting ants and whip the ants away with stinging nettles. Finally, he would take part in foot races and listen to his elders' wisdom.

Young men of the Plains tribes were likewise obliged to go on Vision Quests. The youth would cleanse himself in the sweatbath and then go off alone for several days — sometimes into dark pits or caves — to fast and pray until he had a dream or experienced a vision in which he received instructions from an animal or spirit. The spirit in his vision was believed to be the youth's spiritual guardian, and from then on, he would adopt it as his personal symbol, to be invoked for protection in battle and help in time of need. After the vision, the youth would return home and tell fellow tribe members of his experience. In some tribes, men repeated their Vision Quests as adults whenever they needed special guidance. Once a young man had successfully completed his Vision Quest (and success was not assured on the first try), he was considered ready to join the hunt. The product of his first kill was given to the needy and elderly. Some tribes believed that manhood was achieved with this first successful hunt. A boy initiated into manhood could assemble a medicine bag, a pouch of tools and spiritually significant objects that he brought into battle for protection. If, for example, he had seen an eagle during his Vision Quest, his medicine bag might include an eagle feather. Young men of the Northeast Woodlands also undertook Vision Quests, as a requirement for going to war. Because hunting and warfare

ABOVE: Girls' rites of passage were different from, but no less important than, those of boys. Among the Hopi, when a girl was deemed marriageable, she would style her hair in squash-blossom fashion to signal her availability. Here, a group of Hopi girls, their hair in squash-blossom style, watch the tribal Snake Dance in the city of Walpi in a photo by Edward S. Curtis.

RIGHT: This young woman at Oraibi in Arizona wears her hair in squash-blossom style.

were the chief men's occupations in many tribes, boys' coming of age rites were often linked to either activity.

In other tribes, puberty rites were simply tests of endurance. In the Southwest, the Mojave and Yuma tribes were nomadic hunters and foragers. At puberty, boys had their noses pierced with cords. Then they spent four days running for miles, sleeping and eating only minimally. On the fourth day of this test, a rod replaced the cord and later a bead ornament replaced the rod. Young men of the Northeast Woodlands performed a ritual that required throwing themselves against rocks hard enough to draw blood. Elders who witnessed this act would then name the youth's guardian spirit.

Some puberty rituals took place in conjunction with a tribe's major seasonal festivals. The Southwestern peoples conducted a whole cycle of events associated with the Kachinas, spirits linked with cycles of life and death and the all-important rain. Throughout this cycle, ceremonies featured costumed dancers representing the various Kachinas. These ceremonies included coming of age rites for the young people of the community. Between the ages of five and nine, all boys and some girls underwent Kachina induction, which was achieved by means of a ritual flogging. At the age of fourteen, young men were flogged again, for induction into their fathers' fraternal societies.

During the Sun Dance of the Great Plains, young men underwent painful endurance tests. A sacred tree trunk was an important element of the dance. The young man would tie ropes attached to wooden skewers to the sacred trunk and pierce his chest with the skewers. He would then dance around the trunk until the skewers broke his skin. In another version of this test, the young men wore dry sunflower seeds on their wrists. An elder would light them and the youths would allow the seeds to burn down to the skin. Those who could not tolerate the pain faced the mockery of the group. In still another endurance test, young men competed to see who could get the worst sunburn, or chapped breast. The winner would lead the Chapped Breast Dance.

BELOW: This tanned calf hide was worn by a Sioux girl during her coming of age ceremony in about 1880. It is decorated with quillwork and tufted red yarn.

BELOW: While in many tribes, marriage ceremonies were simple affairs, in others, they could be quite complex. Among the Kwakiutl of the Northwest, the groom arrived by boat with a dancer dressed as a thunderbird, as shown in this photo by Edward S. Curtis.

RIGHT: An Uinta Ute warrior and his bride, photographed in Utah in 1874 by John K. Hillers. Among the Utes, the husband typically joined his wife's family.

Girls took endurance tests of a different sort. Southern California and Southwestern tribes had their young girls lie in a bed of warm sand without speaking or moving for long periods of time. Pueblo and Apache girls endured this for four days; they had to lie face down on the heated sand under a blanket listening to the speeches of their elders. During this time they observed silence and food restrictions; nor could they touch their heads except with special sticks for scratching. During this rite, Apache girls were sprinkled with pollen by older women to promote fertility. Girls of the California tribes also had to swallow tobacco pellets to prove their virtue. Sand painting ceremonies and foot races followed their tests, after which the girls received tattoos. In central California, young people of both sexes had to lie still while their elders cut their backs with blades.

The Hopi girl at puberty spent four days grinding corn in a darkened room to demonstrate her domestic skills. When she had successfully performed this task, an older woman would wash her hair and style it in what was called the open squash blossom style, a public notice that she was ready for marriage. After marriage, her hair would be braided or styled in two rolls to represent the pollinated blossom. Hairstyles figured in other puberty rituals for girls. Among the Plains and Great Basin tribes, when a girl had her first menstrual period, she was the center of a ritual and feast hosted by her parents. At this event, the medicine man instructed her in her duties as

FAR LEFT: A newly married Chippewa couple sits together, accompanied by another couple, on a hillside in 1869. In some tribes, weddings were informal.

ABOVE: Marriage between tribes was common, a result of trade, migrations due to climate changes or epidemics, inter-tribal alliances or warfare in which prisoners were captured. This photo, taken by John K. Hillers in 1879, depicts the household of Tota, a member of the Hopi tribe, who married a Zuñi woman.

39

a woman and to acknowledge her new status publicly, he put an eagle feather in her hair. In the Nootka tribe of the Northwest Coast, young girls wore special hair ornaments during their puberty ceremonies. After these festivities, a young woman was isolated from the community during her menstrual periods, which the tribe associated with evil spirits. During this isolation, her mother instructed her in beadwork, quillwork and other womanly crafts.

Puberty was also feted with feasts and celebrations. In California, where basketry was an art form, women made ceremonial baskets to celebrate girls' arrival at puberty. A girl's first menstrual period was celebrated with dancing. Boys' puberty rites took the form of ceremonies with no women in attendance.

Each tribe had its own marriage customs. Many cultures were divided into clans and moieties. Clans were extended-family groups; marriage within them was often taboo. In the moiety system, a community was divided into two groups, each with different ceremonial responsibilities. The different cultures devised various rules for marriage between moieties; in some, it was proscribed. In California, as the concept of wealth became more popular, rich families developed a preference for marrying each other; this created social classes.

In quite a few tribes, the groom had to give the bride's parents gifts, typically horses. In some cases, such as in the Sub-Arctic, he dedicated a year to hunting for them. In the Southwest, among the Navajo, tradition called for the groom to weave the bride's wedding clothes. In northern California, a string of dentalium shells called a *kaia* was required as a dowry. Bridegrooms of the Northeast Woodlands, California, as well as the Apaches of the Southwest did not speak to their mothers-in-law, in the belief that this maintained family peace.

Polygamy was commonplace in many tribes. On the Plains, men could have several wives, particularly after the coming of the horse, because a mounted hunter who could kill more buffalo needed more help to process the meat. Among the Southeastern tribes, a man could have as many wives as he could provide for. In the southern part of the Great Basin, small family groups traveled by themselves in search of food, and marriages were therefore arranged by families. It was common for a man to marry sisters as well as his brother's widow. Sub-Arctic men could have several wives; in some cases, men shared wives. A wife was considered fair game for wagers and could be lost to another man in a wrestling match. Spousal exchange was not uncommon.

ABOVE: A Seminole woman, wearing the typical patterned cloth dress of her tribe, with her child. The Seminoles were a hybrid group of southeastern tribes and runaway slaves who settled in Florida.

In the Arctic, with its shortage of females, women could have two husbands, although the second might play the role of a servant. Because of the same shortage, marriages were often arranged. Men of the Arctic could likewise have several wives, and in some cases, would steal other men's spouses. It was considered good manners to loan a wife's sexual services to a guest. Close friends also shared their wives, and any resulting children were to be raised by the woman's official husband.

In many cultures, marriage was an informal arrangement. In the Northeast Woodlands, a couple set up housekeeping, often in the wife's home. If a divorce was necessary, the couple simply parted, with the woman retaining the home and custody of the children. In the Southeast, older women of the tribe arranged marriages, although couples had the final say. A man had to prove he could provide a home for his bride before marriage. Marriage was preceded by a year-long trial cohabitation. If the relationship was intact at the year's end, the couple was considered married. In the Arctic, there was no marriage ceremony; a young man in his teens came to live with the family of a young woman and when a child was born, the marriage was considered official.

Formal acknowledgment of marriage did take place on the Northwest Coast, where potlatches — feasts at which the host gave lavish gifts to his guests — were conducted to celebrate all major occasions including puberty, engagements, marriages and countless other events.

North American Indians regarded death in light of their overall views of the universe. For many tribes, life and death was an ongoing cycle. Some cultures believed in reincarnation; others favored the idea of transmigration into other life forms. Still others believed the soul moved on to another world, which, depending on the culture's principal occupation, took different forms.

Many peoples of North America feared death as contagious — or as an entree for dangerous spirits. On the Great Plains, lingering near the dead was deemed risky because the dead were believed to like company. As a result, funerals tended to be simple. In the Great Basin, death was also feared, and it was not unusual for the dying to be abandoned. In the Northeast, some tribes believed death caused illness in the living. Arctic peoples followed death rituals strictly, in the belief that if the dead were not shown proper respect, they would become unfriendly spirits.

The hard lives of many cultures made frailty and old age a liability. Mobility could determine

BELOW: At a Chippewa gravesite photographed in 1858 by H.L. Hime, the grave is covered with sticks and protected by fences.

RIGHT: Plains tribes sometimes provided protection for the corpse by elevating it off the ground. Here, a Sioux gravesite in North Dakota.

ABOVE: In life, Chief Joseph, the leader of the Nez Percé, struggled to maintain peace, but in the face of the U.S. government's insistence on appropriating the tribe's land, was finally forced to lead his people in a doomed rebellion.

whether or not an entire tribe had enough to eat. Young warriors of the Great Plains were taught that it was better to die in battle than grow old. Those who did live to old age were killed or left behind on the trail if they could not keep up with the community. Older people in the Arctic were also abandoned, especially when food was scarce.

None of this meant that those left bereaved were inured to loss. Death at any age was occasion for grief, which was expressed in a variety of ways. On the Plains, women cropped their hair and cut their bodies with knives. In the Great Basin, bereaved spouses mourned for a full year. In the Southwest, after cremation, the bereaved spent four days fasting. In California, after a year, the mourners used reeds, skins and hair to make life-sized figures representing their dead loved ones and spent a week grieving over them, after which the figures were burned. The Inuit sang over the deceased's burial site and brought a ceremonial drink of water there for forty days after the death. The Aleutians, the inhabitants of the temperate islands off the coast of Alaska, mourned for up to sixty days; some observed dietary taboos or gave away their possessions during this time, while others chose the ultimate mourning gesture and killed themselves in order to join their loved ones.

As for the disposal of the dead, that, too, took varied forms. On the Plains, the corpse was set on a raised scaffold out of reach of coyote. A Plains warrior's horse or dog might be killed at graveside. In the Southwest, California, the Great Basin and the Northwest Coast, the deceased were cremated and often their property was burned, as well. The Delaware, an Algonquin tribe, buried their dead in shallow graves to allow their souls to move to the spirit world with ease. For the Inuit, burial was difficult in the Arctic winter, so the dead were covered up as best the grieving family could manage. In some cases, the Arctic peoples placed the corpses of their loved ones in special compartments attached to their homes. On the Northwest Coast, disposal of the deceased's possessions was the job of members of the opposite moiety, and the family of the dead person offered thanks and payment at a potlatch.

Besides burial and cremation, there were other alternatives for the disposal of corpses. These were often reserved for important persons. Some Northwest Coast shamans were mummified, as were shamans and other prominent persons of the Arctic. Corpses of the chiefs of the Northeast Woodlands were preserved in special buildings overseen by priests.

FAR LEFT: *Chief Shuky (or Chief Shakes) of the Tlingit, a Northwest Coast tribe, lying in state at Fort Wrangell, Alaska, after his death in 1879.*

SUSTENANCE

The search for food was a constant in most North American Indians' lives. In this, they differed from their European counterparts who, with the Bronze and Iron Age discoveries of the myriad uses of metal, organized into specialties; some people spent their days as metalsmiths and craftsmen, while others continued to work the land. Among the Indians of North America, specialization was limited. In some tribes, priests and shamans specialized in healing and matters of the spirit, and in others, individuals excelled in various handcrafts, but throughout the continent, most people devoted themselves to obtaining food and outfitting themselves with appropriate shelter and tools. The nature of this work varied from region to region, depending on the local climate, topography and food resources.

The Indians of North America were hunters, gatherers and farmers or a combination of these three. Virtually all the tribes were hunters and gatherers. They foraged for nuts, seeds, berries, roots and wild plants and hunted large and small game animals, birds, sea mammals and fish. These foods took on varying degrees of importance, depending on their availability in a given locale.

Tribes in some regions were foragers first. In California, for example, food was plentiful and the acorn was the staple. Bitter with tannic acid when raw, it had to be ground and soaked before it could be boiled as a cereal or baked into cakes. Another California staple was grass seed, which was ground and mixed with water to make cereal. Some California tribes collected the honeydew of aphids and molded it into pellets. They also gathered and ate clover. All of these foods were supplemented by the region's ample fish and game. By contrast, the people of the Great Basin's southern sector foraged because they had few alternatives. They traveled from place to place in search of food, eating lizards, snakes, insects and jack rabbits. The roots they gathered were a major source of nourishment. When white settlers saw these tribes digging roots they mocked them as "Digger Indians," not realizing that digging was an ingenious means of survival. In the more fertile northern section of the Great Basin, the camas bulb, similar to that of the hyacinth, was common, and some tribes ate lily seeds *(wokas)* as a staple. *Kouse,* also known as biscuit root, was popular among the tribes that lived near the Columbia River. In drier areas, the prickly pear made a good meal.

Another form of foraging presented itself to the Algonquin tribes who inhabited both the western sectors of the Northeast Woodlands and the southern stretches of the Sub-Arctic; they were unique in their use of wild rice, which they harvested by canoe, tapping the grains into the canoe's bottom. Along with other tribes of the Northeast, they also took advantage of the abundant maple groves of the region and used maple sap to make maple sugar, which flavored many a dish.

The Indians of the Northeast, Southeast, Southwest and the Great Plains became farmers, learning to propagate crops from wild seeds. The continent's chief crops were corn, beans and squash, a trio that the Iroquois of the Northeast called the Three Sisters. According to tradition, these three spirit maidens could be seen roaming the fields at night. The tribes of the east could rely largely on rainfall to nourish their crops, but Zuñi, Hopi and Pueblo tribes of the arid Southwest had to become adept at irrigation. Because some of their ancestors had migrated north from the technologically sophisticated cultures of Mexico, they were masters of the gravity-based systems that made the desert bloom.

Throughout the continent, most tribes hunted — large and small game on land, and sea mammals and fish on the water. In places such as the frigid forests of the Sub-Arctic and the desolate inland areas of the Arctic, hunting was often the chief source of food. Tribes in these

ABOVE: A Navajo mother and daughter tend a field on their reservation in this 1939 photo.

RIGHT: Corn, beans and squash were the principal crops of Indian farmers from the Northeast to the Southwest. John K. Hillers photographed pumpkins growing in front of a Zuñi family's adobe home in 1879.

RIGHT: Corn was more than just food; it was a sacred crop to many Southwestern tribes, who used cornmeal in their rituals. Here, a Navajo shelter overlooks a cornfield near Holbrook, Arizona, in an 1889 photo by F.A. Ames.

FAR RIGHT, ABOVE: Fish and other marine life were a key source of nutrition for many tribes, who fished with nets, spears and clubs. Here, a Kwakiutl man catches an octopus.

FAR RIGHT, BELOW: In the often-frozen Arctic, the Inuit peoples had to cut holes in the ice in order to fish. Here, two fishermen pose with a large catch of eels that they had netted through the ice. Because eels traveled slowly, the fishermen had time to send runners to the neighboring village to alert fishermen there to the eels' path.

areas followed the caribou, the mainstay of the diet, which they supplemented with buffalo, moose, bighorn sheep, rabbit, fish and wildfowl when they were available. Totally dependent on the welfare and movements of migratory herds, these peoples lived with the constant possibility of famine. Elsewhere, hunting was key to a mixed diet. Deer was prevalent throughout the continent. In the Northeast, hunters also brought home waterfowl and moose, while in the Southeast, they bagged wild turkey, opossum and bear. In the northern sector of the Great Basin, elk, rabbit, beaver, and other animals were plentiful, while in the southern region, jack rabbit and the occasional antelope were the chief mammalian prey. The peoples of the Northwest Coast, the northern Basin and sections of the Arctic feasted on salmon. Coastal Arctic tribes also hunted whale, sea lion and walrus.

On the Plains and in parts of the Great Basin, buffalo was the primary foodstuff. The tribes of the more fertile eastern Plains divided their time between agriculture and hunting, while those on the western Plains were largely meat eaters. Before the arrival of the horse, the men hunted on foot, luring the buffalo into corrals with fire, stampeding them over cliffs or shooting them with bow and arrow. Once the horse was introduced to North America by the Spanish conquistadors, hunting was easier; mounted hunters surrounded a herd and shot it with bows and arrows and later, with European guns. Women, too, rode horseback and easily hauled away slaughtered animals with travois hitched to the horses.

Plant foods could be dried and stored, but hunting cultures, especially those of the Plains, Great Basin and Sub-Arctic, were faced with the problem of preserving their excess kill. They solved this problem by making pemmican, a ground meat pulp mixed with marrow and other ingredients such as berries. Flattened and dehydrated, it was the ideal food for nomadic peoples. When the time came to eat, it was rehydrated in boiling water. This could be accomplished in several ingenious ways. Before the invention of pottery and its spread in inter-tribal trade, North American Indians often used baskets or internal organs of their larger animal prey as cooking vessels.

RIGHT: The tribes of the Great Plains depended on the buffalo as their main source of food and they adopted a migratory lifestyle in order to follow the herds, living in portable teepees made of hides. Before the coming of the Europeans, they traveled on foot and used dogs to drag carriers called travois. When the Europeans brought horses and wheeled wagons, the Plains tribes eagerly adopted them. In this 1895 photo, a party of Cheyenne have set up camp to preserve their kill. Drying meat is suspended on a line, along with sausage made of the animal's entrails.

Water and food were boiled in these containers by loading them with rocks that had been heated in the fire.

Wherever they lived and whatever they ate, most North American Indian tribes conducted ceremonies to invoke the aid of the spirit world for abundant harvests and successful hunts. And they practiced traditional food customs, as well. In many places, men were hunters and fishermen, while women stayed close to home as gatherers and farmers.

Hunters often offered prayers before hunting, which ranged from simple invocations to major observances such as the Sun Dance of the Plains. Despite its name, this solemn eight-day ceremony did not involve sun worship; instead, it was intended to offer thanks to the spirit world, ask for blessings and guidance for the future and rally the tribe together for the buffalo hunt. Each tribe had its own interpretation of the ritual, but it often had as its centerpiece a sacred tree trunk decked with greens.

The Sun Dance also included coming of age rituals for the young men of the tribe, who had to perform painful endurance tests. Another coming of age rite was the preparation of the buffalo medicine sausage; young warriors ate it while pronouncing the names of the girls they hoped to marry.

The Sun Dance was important in readying the tribe for the hunt, which required the cooperation of large numbers of people. Some were designated as scouts, some as hunters, some as policemen to keep order, and some as warriors to keep watch for enemies. Immediately after the hunt, the participants helped themselves to a delicacy: raw liver. The women traveled with the men; after the hunt, they butchered the meat and prepared a feast of roast buffalo. Excess meat was dried and preserved as pemmican. The women also prepared other parts of the animal such as the hide, hair, bones and organs, all of which had specific uses. The hump, for example, was shaped and dried to be used as a cooking vessel. The cleaned paunch was also a cooking vessel, an edible one.

The Mandan tribe conducted a Buffalo Dance, in which dancers wore buffalo skins and imitated the movements of the buffalo to lure its spirit nearer to the tribe.

In the northern part of the Great Basin, salmon was key to the diet; the Indians erected platforms over the rivers and fished with nets or spears. Because salmon was such an important

LEFT: Whale was a mainstay of the peoples of the Arctic and parts of the Northwest Coast, as it provided food, skins, bone and blubber. Arctic fishermen offered their catch a ritual drink of water as thanks for providing them with these resources. Here, members of the Makah, a Northwest Coast tribe, butcher a whale. The 1910 photo was taken by Asahel Curtis, a relative of the more famous Edward S. Curtis.

RIGHT: Hopi Indians of Arizona perform the Buffalo Dance in this 1923 photo. The chiefs carried buffalo horns during the dance.

BELOW: Salmon was a major foodstuff of the Northwest Coast Indians. Women were typically not allowed near the fishing areas, but they prepared the catch. Here male and female musicians of the Makah tribe take part in a Salmon Feast in 1923.

ABOVE: At San Ildefonso Pueblo in New Mexico, buffalo dancers from Acoma Pueblo perform their traditional ceremony.

RIGHT: Members of the Shipavlovi perform a ritual of singing to snakes in preparation for the Snake Dance, in this photo by Edward S. Curtis.

foodstuff, some of the tribes of the Plateau appointed a Salmon Chief who oversaw the fishing operation and thwarted any witchcraft that might be practiced by neighboring tribes. Women were barred from fishing areas for fear that they would spread contamination; however, as in other cultures, they were responsible for preparing and preserving the catch. For the southern Basin tribes, the food supply was so sparse that the small family groups that constituted the basic tribal unit came together in large numbers only for their annual rabbit and antelope hunts, which required many people to string huge mile-long nets across their hunting grounds.

The Inuit followed strict dietary taboos and hunting rituals, which included not mixing the meat of land and sea animals at meals. The spirit world had to be respected, and that meant honoring the animals taken for food. Seals and whales were offered a symbolic drink of water once they were killed, so their spirits would return to the spirit world and pass the word that they had been treated well by the human hunters; this ensured that seals and whales would allow themselves to be killed by human hunters in the future. The hunters carried the water in water-tight mittens that they packed inside their clothing to keep thawed. Likewise, the polar bear was held on the spear that killed it for five days before it could be used. In summertime, families would come together for feasting and a festival of singing, dancing, contests and gambling.

A Messenger Feast took place at the end of the year, when the inland and shore tribes met to celebrate their trade relationship.

Among the Sub-Arctic Indians, some believed in a cannibal demon who possessed those who had been forced to eat the flesh of the dead in times of famine. According to tradition, this demon had to be killed with a stake through the heart. Hunters also sought news of the future by "reading" cracks in animal bones held over a fire.

Farmers too, had their major ceremonies, and these typically involved requests to the spirit world for rain and abundant crop yields. In the Southwest, the Pueblo peoples celebrated a cycle of ceremonies in honor of the group of spirits called Kachinas. These ceremonies invoked the Kachinas' aid for enough rainfall and good crops. The Hopi and Zuñi tribes' major agricultural ceremonies were the solemn Green Corn Dance, as well as the Snake Dance and Flute Dance, which alternated yearly. These rituals also called on the spirit world for rain and abundance. The Snake Dance required men to dance with live snakes — rattlesnakes and others — and clutch them in their mouths, drop them in cornmeal and then release them into the wild to return to the spirit world with news of the tribe's great piety. Cornmeal was considered sacred and was often used during these ceremonies, as well as in healing rituals. Zuñi priests planted feathered sticks in the cornfields to bring rain. Another tradition called for Hopi and Zuñi men to race across planted fields as they wished the rain to do. The young men of the Pueblos of the Rio Grande kicked buckskin bags of corn over the fields until they burst and the kernels spilled out. The Hopi performed a bean dance in late winter to encourage the plants to bloom again, using bean seedlings as part of the ceremony. Another tribe, the Papago, celebrated the saguaro harvest, in honor of a local fig-like fruit. The juice of the saguaro was boiled and allowed to ferment. The men drank it during the ceremony, one of the few in North America to incorporate alcohol.

In the Southeast, the Green Corn Ceremony was an important harvest observance. It marked the new year, a time of house cleaning and ritual purification, fasting and feasting. During this four- to eight-day ritual of renewal, the community's sacred fire was extinguished and replaced with a new flame that would burn for the new year. (A similar fire ritual was performed in the Northeast in midwinter.) Tribe members themselves underwent purification by drinking a "black drink," an herbal emetic.

In the Northeast Woodlands, farming tribes observed a cycle of ceremonies in honor of various crops, from the strawberries of spring to the Great Corn Festival of the harvest season.

The Northwest Coastal Indians lived in what has been called the most generous environment of the entire continent, and as a result, they spent less time than some of their neighbors in the quest for food. Although the climate would have been ideal for agriculture, there was no need for it; abundant game, fish and wild plants left them free for other pursuits. Their major ceremony was the potlatch, a great feast at which the host had the chance to show off his wealth by feeding his guests extravagantly and giving them lavish gifts. This ceremony was also conducted farther north in the Arctic, where it took on new importance; in time of famine and food scarcity, it was a means of redistributing food from those who had it to those who did not.

DAILY LIFE

Local environmental conditions determined how the North American Indian peoples lived; various styles of shelter, clothing, tools and decorative items were a tribe's response to what the land had to give. But these things were rarely geared to function alone. Form was important, and everything from the most modest tool to the most sacred ceremonial object was likely to be decorated according to a tribe's spiritual beliefs and sense of aesthetics. Within the limitations set by nature and by their own Stone Age orientation, North American Indians devised ingenious and varied answers to the basic questions of survival. And as with peoples all over the world, invention and habit gave rise to tradition.

The local climate was, of course, a good predictor of the kinds of shelter that tribes would fashion for themselves, but not completely; so were the local food resources that particular tribes chose to adopt. Not surprisingly, harsher weather required stronger structures. Beyond that, nomadic tribes who followed the movements of herds, the spawning paths of fish or the seasonal growth of wild vegetation needed shelter that was easy to assemble and easy to carry. Farmers who stayed put to tend crops had more substantial and permanent lodgings. Tribes who did both often had two sets of shelter, one permanent and one portable. All over the continent, North American Indian cultures created wooden framed structures covered with bark, earth,

mud, grass, reeds, thatch or hides. Some were partially underground to take advantage of added warmth or coolness that the earth afforded. Others, in warmer climates, were open-sided. Many were multi-family dwellings that housed a clan or large group. Tribes of the Northeast Woodlands, the Southeast, the Great Basin, the Sub-Arctic, California and parts of the Southwest all developed variations on these themes. Other tribes built shelter that was quite different.

In the frozen Arctic, some Inuit peoples made use of ice, the very substance that made their surroundings so threatening and their food supply so limited. With ice blocks arranged in a spiral formation and held together with snow, they built igloos, sometimes far out over the frozen seas. When heated by an indoor fire, igloos could be quite warm. In summer, the Inuit moved inland to hunt and fish. There, they lived in lodges covered with sod, sealskin or caribou skin. Whale bones were used for frames and whale gut for windows.

In the rainy forests of the Northwest Coast, the local peoples became master woodworkers and carvers. Longhouses were made of wooden planks put together by means of tongue-in-groove construction. Cedar shingles lined the outside of these buildings. Floors were planked and the houses were divided into rooms so that they could accommodate large numbers of people. The biggest were as long as 100 feet. Great fishermen, the Northwest Coast Indians built their houses facing the sea. They did make seasonal forays inland for hunting and gathering, but always returned to their seaside homes. The use of wooden planks set the Northwest Coast Indians apart from other peoples in North America, but even more singular was their fondness for elaborate totem carvings. These fantastical representations of birds, animals and spirits associated with the occupants' clans were built into the frame of every home, and after the 1800s, they took the form of free-standing poles, some as tall as fifty feet. The facade carvings were often open-mouthed, with the mouth serving as the door of the house. These totems were not religious in nature, but were more like a clan's coat-of-arms.

Even bigger than the wooden houses of the Northwest Coast were the adobe and stone buildings of the Southwest Pueblo Indians. Because they tended large farms, the Pueblos were sedentary peoples who lived in permanent villages. The adobe complex was often several stories high and could be divided into hundreds of apartments — much like a modern apartment building. The first of these structures were built by the vanished cultures of the Anasazi and their con-

LEFT: In Yakutat Bay, Alaska, seal skins are stretched on frames to dry at a Tlingit seal hunters' encampment of bark-covered huts. Because of its water-resistant qualities, Arctic peoples used seal skin in a variety of ways, for clothing, tools, shelter and boats.

temporaries, who lived hundreds of years before Christ. They built their apartment blocks
both on the ground and on the cliffs, earning the posthumous name Cliff Dwellers from archaeologists. Those who came later, the Hopi, Zuñi and Pueblo tribes and others, continued to use
adobe materials for their homes.

That a people's occupation determined its housing style can be seen by comparing
the Hopi, Zuñi and Pueblo tribes with their Navajo neighbors. The latter were horsemen, sheep
herders and hunters who did a limited amount of farming. They lived in far smaller communities
of simple domed hogans — eight-sided wood frames covered with earth or brush. New encampments could be constructed quickly if migration was necessary.

The peoples of the Great Plains followed the migratory buffalo herds, so their shelter,
too, had to be easily portable. The buffalo provided them with a solution: the teepee, a cone-
shaped tent made of tanned buffalo hides stretched over several poles. The teepee was transport-
ed on a travois, a carrier without wheels that was dragged by people or dogs, and later by horses.
(Similar hide-covered shelters were used by the Athapascans of the Sub-Arctic, who followed
the caribou.) On the eastern Plains, where the people farmed for part of the year and hunted for
the rest, the teepee provided shelter during hunting season only; these peoples returned several
times a year to permanent villages of log-framed earthen lodges for planting and harvesting.

Clothing, too, was a result of climate and available resources. The uniform of many tribes
consisted of buckskin loincloths for men and aprons or wrap-around skirts for women. Leggings

BELOW: The Navajos were known for their intricate weaving. Early weavers used vegetable dyes, but when Spanish traders brought deep red English flannel to the region, that color became popular. Weavers unraveled the flannel and rewove it with their other colored fibers into new blankets and garments. Here, a bright Navajo poncho.

RIGHT: Most North American Indians wore loose-fitting animal-skin garments. Here, a woman's beaded and painted moose-hide dress from the Sub-Arctic Cree people.

FAR RIGHT: An Inuit girl's coat of caribou skin, fur and beads. Heavy clothing, tailored close to the body was required to survive the Arctic cold, but it did not go unadorned.

 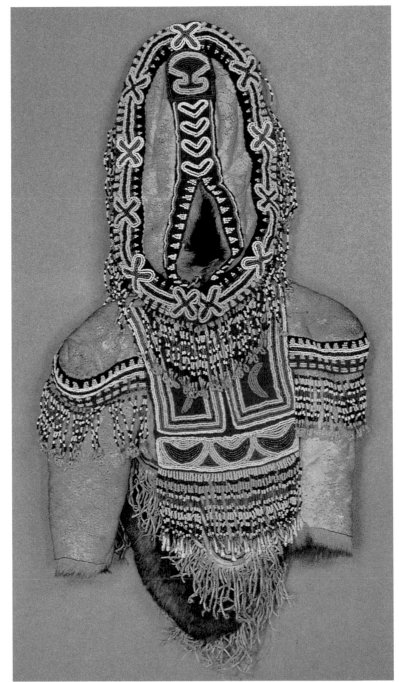

and shirts or ponchos, and for women, one-piece dresses, were worn for added warmth. Robes of buffalo or other fur offered protection from severe cold. Heavy walking required moccasins or boots, but some peoples wore sandals or went barefoot.

Much North American Indian clothing was made of animal skin, but cloth was also used. Southwest peoples grew cotton and wove it into cloth for lightweight clothing, blankets (which often doubled as clothing) and rugs; the Navajos became famous for their colorful weaving. Northwest Coast tribes wove wool from mountain goats and bighorn sheep into blankets. When European traders brought broadcloth and calico and manufactured blankets, other tribes eagerly adopted the new fabrics and the European fashions that came with them. Trade cloth and blankets were embraced as labor-saving advances and were acquired in return for furs.

Extremes of climate required special adaptations. The Inuit needed warm, waterproof clothing, so they fashioned waterproof parkas and boots out of sealskin and seals' internal organs. Fur-trimmed hoods kept their heads warm. Unlike the loose fashions of most North American Indians, Arctic clothing had to be tailored to the body to keep out the wind. Some tribes favored suits of polar bear or squirrel fur, which they layered for warmth. Another style was the anorak, with long tails in back, which made sitting on cold surfaces more comfortable. The inclement weather of the Northwest Coast made broad-brimmed hats fashioned out of roots and capes made of bark very practical.

Especially for ceremonial occasions, Indian peoples throughout North America liked to trim their clothing and items such as quivers, cradleboards and pouches with sewn-on decorations. Originally, this meant shells, seeds, animal hair, animal teeth and claws and porcupine quills, all of which required hours of preparation and meticulous handwork, done largely by women. The Europeans brought beads made of Venetian glass, which made decorating clothes infinitely easier and increased the range and brightness of colors available. Unlike shell beads and other traditional trimmings, Venetian glass beads were pre-pierced and could be sewn onto a garment with ease. Metal needles acquired in trade and substituted for bone awls made the work even easier. Traditional beadwork patterns tended to be geometric and angular. When an order of Ursuline nuns established itself in Quebec in the 1600s, they taught the women of the local tribes French embroidery techniques. Soon, rounded shapes and floral patterns were

BELOW: A Nez Percé hide dress is trimmed with beads, fringe, cowrie shells and bells. The floral design is likely to have originated with Ursuline nuns who taught northeastern tribes, who in turn passed the designs west.

BELOW RIGHT: This buffalo-hide belt pouch from the Crow tribe of the Plains and Prairies dates from the 1840s. It is trimmed with tin cones, horse hair and beads in colorful geometric patterns.

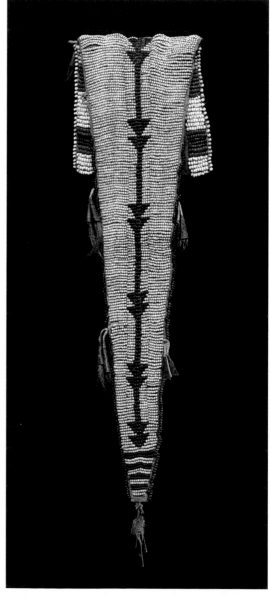

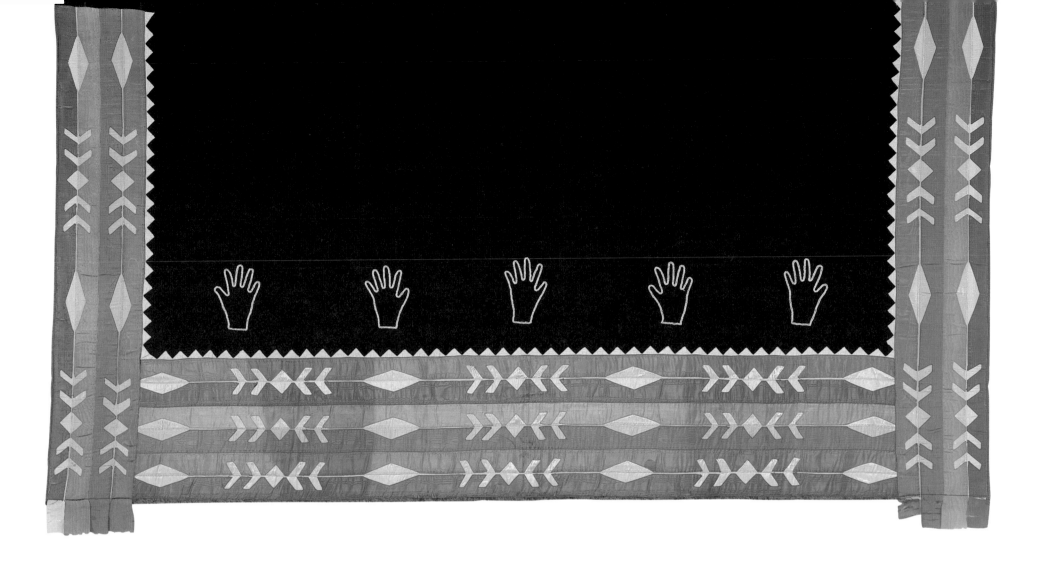

introduced to other regions through trade between tribes.

All over the continent and particularly in the Arctic, Northeast Woodlands, Southwest, California and Northwest Coast, tribes favored tattoos and body paint for ceremonial or everyday use. Tattoos and body paint could signal a girl's availability for marriage or a warrior's achievement in battle. Individuals often looked to dreams for inspiration in their designs.

Body piercing was also popular. Earrings were a common adornment in many places; Plains newborns had their tiny ears pierced. Southwestern, Great Basin, Northwest Coast, Arctic and Sub-Arctic tribes favored nose piercing; for Mojave and Yuma boys of the desert Southwest, it was part of the puberty ritual. Lip piercing was also practiced, especially in the Arctic and by the tribes of the Northwest Coast.

ABOVE: A "wearing" blanket from the Osage tribe of the Plains and Prairies region is made of black wool trade cloth, trimmed with ribbon appliqués and decorated with five beaded hands. It dates from the 1890s.

Tools, carriers, ornaments and other possessions reflected the available resources of each area and the needs, aspirations and imaginations of the tribes who made them. Gatherers, for example, needed carriers so they could transport and store their seeds, berries and other prizes. Baskets, either woven or made of sewn coils, were lightweight, portable carriers, and with straps and handles, left the gatherer's hands free for work. Pouches and bags often served the same purpose. Digging sticks and seed beaters were among the other tools used for gathering. Hunting required its own tools: spears, bows and arrows, clubs, nets, snares, fish hooks and harpoons, to name a few. The *atlatl* was widely used to add more propulsion to an ordinary spear. Farmers used hoes made of stone and bone; buffalo shoulder blades proved to be ideal hoes.

Throughout the continent, without the aid of the wheel and before the coming of the horse, transportation of goods required a major effort. In this, North America's natural waterways proved an invaluable resource. Tribes from many regions built boats: bark-covered canoes were typical in the Northeast Woodlands, the Great Basin and the Sub-Arctic; kayaks and larger whalebone-and-skin umiaks in the Arctic; wooden dugouts in the Southeast and the Great Basin; large wooden canoes in the Northwest Coast and reed rafts and wooden-plank boats in the Southwest and California.

On land, the travois, a carrier dragged on the ground, made the travels of the tribes of the Plains and surrounding areas much easier. In the Arctic, dogsleds were invaluable for moving across the frozen landscape.

Most tribes had tools for making fires. A simple pair of stones or a "drill" twirled to make a spark usually sufficed. The knife was another basic tool, used for cutting food, skinning animals and shaping tools. A variety of other blades of stone and shell were used for shaving and shaping wood and other cutting jobs. Cordage, important for fastening and for fishing and hunting nets, was made of bark, roots, buckskin and rolled grass, hay or animal sinew.

Some implements were specific to individual culture areas. Southwestern Indians became masters of pottery making. With coils of clay smoothed to perfection, they created pots of all sizes and decorated them with geometric patterns and figures in many colors. The Navajos gained fame not only for their blanket weaving, but also for their jewelry. In the 1800s, they learned the art of making silver jewelry and ornaments from their Mexican neighbors and became expert

RIGHT: This Acoma Pueblo ceramic jar dates from about 1890. Bird motifs were common on Acoma whiteware, as birds were believed to be a link between heaven and earth.

FAR RIGHT, ABOVE: Baskets were an important item for the North American Indians, most of whom did at least some foraging for food. Hop pickers near Puget Sound in Washington use large baskets in this photo by Edward S. Curtis.

FAR RIGHT, BELOW: Baskets were not merely practical; they were also an art form, as this covered basket from the Makah tribe of the Northwest Coast illustrates. The whaling motif illustrates the importance of the whale to the Makah.

silversmiths. Silver and turquoise became a traditional combination. The squash blossom, a significant motif throughout the Southwest, was often integrated into jewelry designs.

Arctic peoples carved tools and ceremonial objects from ivory, a byproduct of two of their main food sources: whale and walrus. They carved these designs to release any spirits trapped inside the ivory. The carver would listen to the wind pass over the piece and carve what he "heard." The Inuit created many tools to deal with their harsh climate, including snow knives, snow goggles, probes for finding thin ice, thimbles, stone oil lamps (wood was too scarce to burn), shovels, dogsleds, barbed fish spears, harpoons, pestles, chisels, and kayaks.

Likewise, the buffalo performed a vital function for the peoples of the Plains; besides eating buffalo meat as their main form of nourishment and tanning hides for teepees, they also used hides for clothing, blankets, pouches and shields; buffalo hair for weaving; and horns, hoofs and bones for making tools and utensils. Inner organs became cooking vessels; sinews made cordage, rope and bow string; and tails were fashioned into fly swatters. Even buffalo excrement was used, as fuel.

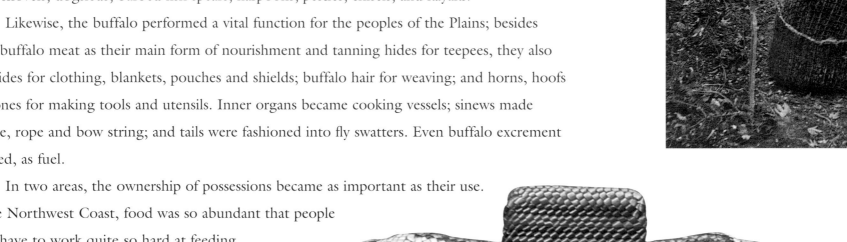

In two areas, the ownership of possessions became as important as their use. On the Northwest Coast, food was so abundant that people didn't have to work quite so hard at feeding themselves and they had more time for other pursuits. Chief among them were wood-working and carving. Northwest Coast peoples designed a variety of tools for woodworking — wedges for splitting planks, beaver tooth chisels and knives — and with them, made cradles, rattles, platters, pots and more. In addition to the giant totem poles that decorated their homes, they carved similar figures on their canoes, storage containers, beds, bowls, utensils and tools. There was plenty of time, too, for

ABOVE: Waterways were North America's highways, and boats were important for both transport and fishing. Here, a three-hatch skin boat and the frame of another in Knicklick, Prince William Sound, Alaska, in a photo by Merle LaVoy.

RIGHT: Fire-starting implements were basic to any North American Indian tool kit. Some rubbed stones together, while others, like the Apache pair shown in this photo by Edward S. Curtis, used fire drills.

amassing these possessions and art objects. This led to the custom of the potlatch, the feast at which the host gave away his possessions to his guests to prove his wealth. Potlatches were held to celebrate many occasions — a child's puberty rites, marriage, mourning for a loved one, a memorial for ancestors — but the format was always the same: lavish gift-giving by the host. Copper plaques became prized souvenirs. Potlatch attendees wore special hats that could be fitted with discs to denote the number of potlatches given by the wearer. As time went on, potlatches became competitive, and hosts all but bankrupted themselves to demonstrate their wealth. Some ended their potlatches by burning any leftover goods or throwing them into the sea. But they usually regained at least some of this lost wealth, because their guests were obliged to match and even outdo them with their own potlatches.

The collection of wealth also preoccupied the peoples of California. These tribes, especially the Pomo, were expert basket-makers. They wove willow and various kinds of roots and bark into geometric patterns and decorated their baskets with shells and feathers. Baskets were given as gifts for special events. Others were made as burial goods. The California peoples also favored dentalium shells strung as necklaces, collars, and used as clothing decorations. These beads were used as dowries, to settle arguments and as currency for trade. Unlike their Northwest Coast neighbors, California peoples passed their accumulated wealth from one generation to the next. Oversized knives made of obsidian were favorite collectibles and were carried with pride during the White Deerskin Dance. This was one of the two dances of the sacred World Renewal Ceremony, and it offered an opportunity to show off. Dancers carried poles bearing deerskins with the heads and antlers still on; white skins of albino deer were the most prized. The dancers wore shell necklaces, feathered head-dresses and ornaments of sea lion teeth.

WAR AND PEACE

North American Indians have been stereotyped as savage warriors and romanticized as peace-loving naïfs. In truth, they were neither; they were both and much more, just like any complex collection of cultures.

Warfare became a struggle for survival only when Europeans and later, United States settlers began to push the North American Indians off their land. But war had always been a feature of many tribes' lives and there were countless ceremonies and traditions to go along with it. In a few tribes, war and its aftermath could be quite brutal; prolonged torture and sacrifice of prisoners was common. Elsewhere, scalping, learned from the European invaders, became a military custom. Still other tribes took prisoners, either as slaves or to be adopted into their captors' communities.

But brutality was very often beside the point. Although many North American Indian tribes made war to settle territorial disputes or to avenge blood feuds, for still others, warfare was a sport, much like the jousting of European nobles in the age of chivalry. True, it was a dangerous sport with a high potential for injury and death, but destruction was not the goal. For tribes of the Southeast, the Northeast Woodlands and the Plains, it became more honorable to touch a member of an enemy tribe with a stick called a coup stick than to wound or kill him.

Warriors of the Plains were actually awarded points for various deeds, and touching the enemy with the coup stick brought a high score.

Warfare, for whatever purpose, had its associated rituals and traditions. Young men went to war dressed in special war shirts decorated with quills or beads, human hair, fur and paint; paint was also used to decorate their faces and bodies. Surprise was a key element of warfare. Clubs, stone axes, spears, and bows and arrows were the principal weapons of North American Indian warfare until the arrival of the Europeans, who brought with them metal blades, guns and horses. Once horses arrived, they became both tools and spoils of war. Among the Blackfeet, warriors earned the most points for capturing enemy horses. Throughout the Plains, Great Basin and the Southwest, rivalries developed as tribes competed to accumulate horses and acquire the best hunting grounds. And because the horse made hunting so much more efficient, there was more time for the sport of war.

Regional resources resulted in different military techniques. In the Northwest, tribes staged raids by canoe, and warriors wore protective garments of roots and hide and carried copper daggers in addition to the typical weapons. Southeastern tribes prepared for war with several days of fasting, feasting, body painting and watching carefully for omens. A bad omen was enough to postpone an attack. In the Southwest, warriors used arrows dipped in deer liver that had been mixed with snake venom.

Shields were brought into battle by warriors of many tribes. As Ronald McCoy wrote in his essay "Circles of Power," prehistoric artwork unearthed by archaeologists depicts warriors equipped with full-body shields, but virtually none remain as artifacts. Later shields were smaller, circular affairs made of coiled basketry or smoke-toughened buffalo hide. These afforded good protection from enemy arrows, but after the introduction of firearms, they were of little use against bullets. Those who used the shields, however, believed devoutly that they were imbued with supernatural protective powers and continued to carry them into battle. Decorating a shield properly was thought to strengthen these powers. In the Southwest, images of the sun and of circles, likenesses of the Kachina spirits,

RIGHT: Often, warriors decorated their weapons with symbolic images seen in dreams or prescribed by shamans. This gunstock club from the Shoshoni tribe of the Great Basin dates from about 1860 and is trimmed with tackwork over painted panels.

FAR RIGHT: In some cultures, warriors donned special battle clothes. This deerhide war shirt from the Assiniboine tribe of the Great Plains dates from about 1870, and is painted and trimmed with beads, red trade cloth and ermine drops.

RIGHT: Some warriors favored body paint for battle. Here, Chief Last Horse displays a fierce-looking face on his stomach, in a photo taken in about 1880. He carries a shield and wears a miniature shield around his neck. Shields were thought to be endowed with spirit power that could protect their wearers.

animals and lightning bolts all appeared on shields. Apache warriors decorated their shields, inside and out, with colorful abstract designs to represent lightning, wind, snakes, mountains, stars and planets. On the Plains, where a shield was a warrior's most important possession, decorations reflected the imagery of the warrior's Vision Quest. Lightning, spider webs, thunderbirds, dragonflies, buffalo, and other creatures of nature were typical of the shield art of the Sioux. Charms, feathers, braided grasses and corn husks were often attached to the shields by warriors of many regions. Owl feathers were thought by Sioux warriors to improve night vision, while eagle feathers were associated with strength. In some tribes, warriors matched their warpaint to their shields. The Navajos sprinkled pollen on their shields in the belief that it made them invisible. Among the Cheyenne, members of the Red Shield Warrior Society swung their shields in the air to neutralize their enemies' weapons. Some warriors observed specific dietary taboos that had been revealed in dreams or visions in order not to dissipate their shields' powers. Among the Hopis of the Southwest, shields decorated with likenesses of Kachinas spirits were used in puberty rites, women's ceremonies, in the Buffalo Dance and the winter solstice ceremony.

Once a battle was over, there were many ways to recognize the returning warriors. Apache warriors who killed an enemy spent sixteen days purifying themselves by fasting in seclusion. On the Plains and in the Great Basin, some tribes held dances after battle to mourn their dead and celebrate those who had returned. At these dances, warriors took turns telling of their own bravery. Often, enemy scalps were displayed, in the hope that the powers of the dead would be passed on to the living. The Mojave and Yuma peoples of the Southwest hung scalps on poles and used them in a post-raid dance that lasted for days. Anyone who handled the scalps had to undergo strict cleansing afterward.

On the Plains, feathers were awarded for great deeds and they were marked to show what the wearer had done. The eagle feather headdresses made famous by Hollywood were actually awarded only to heroes; thirty-six feathers constituted a full bonnet. Bonnets were decorated with ribbons, eagle talons, fur and other materials. They were blessed during dances; women were selected to dance wearing them. Some bonnets were subject to dietary taboos, much like those observed for shields. Often, the warrior himself had to procure feathers for his bonnet, and this task could be made more challenging by the requirement that he did not kill the eagle first.

ABOVE: A Navajo warrior carries a lance and shield in this photo taken by James Mooney near Keam's Canyon on the Navajo Reservation in 1892. Shields afforded good protection against arrows and lances, but were of little use against white men's bullets; still, many warriors continued to carry them because they believed in their spiritual powers.

FAR LEFT: This 19th century buffalo-hide shield from Acoma Pueblo bears painted images of a bird, probably an eagle, stars and snakes.

LEFT: This Apache shield of buffalo rawhide dates from about 1880. Its painted cover depicts thunder, lightning and a thunderbird.

ABOVE: This colorful buffalo-hide shield from the Kiowa people of the Plains dates from about 1860. A deerhide apron trimmed with tin cones is draped over it.

Another headdress of the Plains and Great Basin was the splithorn bonnet, made of bison horns and trimmed with fur and feathers.

Peace, too, had its rituals and arrangements. Some were practical. Against the ravages of the Spanish conquistadors, some Pueblo peoples found refuge with their Navajo rivals. They brought with them their knowledge of agriculture and their religion, both of which the Navajos adopted. In the Northeast Woodlands, Iroquois leaders, tired of endless blood feuds, organized the Iroquois Confederacy to settle disputes between participating tribes. The peaceful peoples of California did not make war among themselves, which made them an easy target for Northwest Coast slave raiders. Among themselves, they used payment in the form of strings of dentalium shells to settle disputes.

Among the Algonquins of the Northeast Woodlands and the Sub-Arctic, belts made of wampum — shell ground into beads — symbolized treaties between tribes and served as diplomatic credentials for tribal ambassadors. The Algonquins also conducted powwows — feasts with songs, dances and contests to promote friendship. Attendees packed food and gifts for distribution at the powwow into a friendship pouch, a decorated bag made for the occasion.

The peace pipe has been romanticized in the "Western" genre, but it actually was an important ceremonial tool in treaty agreements, especially among tribes of the Northeast Woodlands and the Sub-Arctic. Among these peoples, passing the peace pipe validated treaties. Possession of a peace pipe could, like the wampum belt, serve as a diplomatic credential for travelers. Much of the stone used to make pipes came from a sacred quarry in Minnesota where warfare was forbidden. The quarry's red stone was a valuable trade commodity and it made its way all over the country. Tobacco, considered a sacred crop by many peoples, was cultivated in many places, particularly in the Northeast Woodlands, the Southeast, Southwest, the Great Plains and the Great Basin. Tobacco was used in peace ceremonies and other rituals; smoke was thought to be a medium of communication with the spirit world.

BELOW: An otter fur turban trimmed with beads, ribbon and a buffalo horn made by the Oto, circa 1870. This style was favored by tribes of the western Great Lakes and Prairies.

BELOW RIGHT: Pipes were carried in specially decorated bags. Here, an Arapaho bag, circa 1860 (left) and a Ute bag with stem holder, circa 1870.

RIGHT: This ermine-covered headdress topped with beaded buffalo horns from the Plateau region is a variation of the Plains war bonnet.

FAR RIGHT: A pipe tomahawk from the Great Lakes area, circa 1860, did double duty. The Cheyenne shot pouch, circa 1840, is made of red trade cloth trimmed in beads.

RIGHT: Pipes were traditionally passed to validate peace treaties. At the Oglala Dakota treaty meeting at Fort Laramie, Wyoming, in 1868, a chief smokes the council pipe to mark the significance of the event. The moment was captured on film by Alexander Gardner.

FAR RIGHT: A calumet, or ceremonial pipe, from the Mandan tribe of the Plains and Prairies region. It was obtained by the explorers Lewis and Clark during their expedition of 1804-05.

TRIBAL SOCIETY

Social structure among the many North American Indian nations was as varied as it is among nations today. While most individuals were similarly concerned with procuring the basics of survival, the societies they lived in were organized in many ways. In some cultures, the governing principles were secular, while in others, they were religious; in the Southwest, with its emphasis on strict group coordination for large-scale farming and building, priests wielded the most power. Virtually all cultures supported a class of shamans and healers.

Men held most positions of authority, whether secular or religious, but in some cultures, women exercised considerable power behind the scenes. Except in wealth-obsessed societies of the Northwest Coast and California, women typically owned all household goods — including the house, whatever form it took. Men owned their hunting and battle gear. Among the Iroquois, clan mothers had the power to choose and recall the chiefs who represented the various tribes at the Great Council. They also determined the community planting schedule. Quite a few cultures throughout the continent were matrilineal; power and prestige went to the men, but was passed to them from their mothers.

Politically, the North American cultures were varied. The tiered representative government of the Iroquois was far removed from the rigid social class system of the Northwest Coast,

and neither resembled the family units who wandered the southern region of the Great Basin. On the Great Plains, political structures tended to be informal, as would befit tribes that broke into small hunting groups. Men's societies acted as police and kept order during the hunt, to enable hunters to concentrate on their prey. Other societies were charged with teaching tribal traditions and passing down community history. On the Plains, chiefs were elected based on their deeds in battle, but did not wield much power over the activities of their subjects. In the Great Basin, politics and religion were likewise loosely organized. Village leaders directed the small bands that traveled in search of food. In time of war, the bands selected a war leader.

The Northwest Coast Indians organized into villages and within villages, into clans based on lineage and classes based on wealth. The highest ranking chiefs had their pick of the best fishing areas and other resources. Nobles came next, followed by commoners. Slaves captured in war were considered property that could be used as beasts of burden or killed at will.

Northeast Woodlands tribes had what is often described as the most complex political organizations north of Mesoamerica. The Iroquois, in particular, formed a highly structured confederation known as the Five Nations. Five tribes made up the confederation: the Mohawks, the

LEFT: Northwest Coast tribes lived by strict class hierarchies. Here, a Nakoaktok chief's daughter has a special seat, symbolically supported by the heads of her slaves, at her father's potlatch in this photo by Edward S. Curtis.

ABOVE: Some tribes venerated bears as spiritual beings. Bear's Belly, of the Arikara tribe of the Plains and Prairies, belonged to the spiritual fraternity of Bears because he had been attacked by three bears and killed them all. In this photo by Edward S. Curtis, he wears a bearskin robe.

ABOVE: Elaborate hinged masks were worn during the Winter Dance of the Northwest Coast tribes. In this photo by Curtis, dancers portray mythical birds.

RIGHT: The Ghost Dance was a religious ceremony that developed in the late 1800s in response to white society's relentless westward push and the banishment of the North American Indian to reservations. The dance was a frenzied ceremony in which participants wore fringed muslin shirts that they believed would protect them from white men's bullets. They danced and sang until they lost consciousness and received visions of a happy future. The dance's founder predicted that the Ghost Dance would cause an earthquake or other disaster to swallow up white society, leaving behind its wealth for the Indians, and reuniting them with their ancestors. Instead, the spread of the movement frightened the white authorities and touched off their infamous massacre of some 200 Sioux at Wounded Knee, South Dakota, in 1890. Here, a girl's fringed Ghost Dance dress.

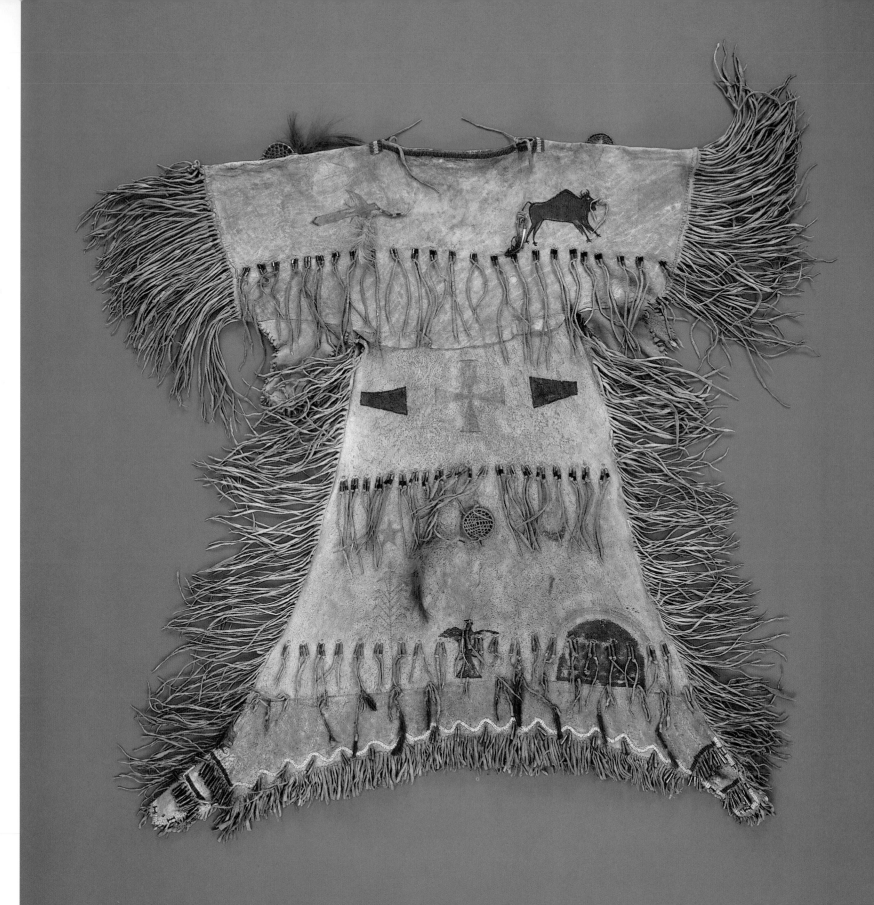

Senecas, the Oneidas, the Onondagas and the Cayugas. Each tribe had its own governing council and each sent representatives to a central council of the confederation, which arbitrated territorial disputes, blood feuds and other disagreements. The other two large Northeast groups, the Algonquin and the Siouan, were not as organized as the Iroquois, but individual tribes devised their own approaches to politics. The Delaware, a branch of the Algonquin group, for example, could only go to war if a council of old and wise men decided to do so. Southeastern tribes organized around the village and each village typically had a council that met daily to consider community issues. Intertribal councils took place among one Southeast tribe, the Creeks. In the Arctic, winter was the time for social and ceremonial dancing. Individuals involved in disputes took advantage of these gatherings to air their arguments, which were expressed in song before the community.

Whatever their political organization, most North American Indian tribes had shamans to serve as healers and facilitate relations with the spirit world. That world was interpreted differently by the various cultures, but most shared the belief that supernatural forces could influence human affairs for good or ill, and that intermediaries — humans with special gifts — could make a difference in the community's fate. Shamans were called on to appease evil spirits and neutralize witchcraft practiced by enemy tribes. Some re-enacted creation stories at community ceremonies. They were also charged with finding lost objects and people, predicting the future, offering benedictions for hunt and harvest and luring herds. In the Arctic, they offered prayers for rescue at sea. In many cultures, shamans and healers experienced a "calling" to their profession in the form of dreams and visions that were believed to be messages from the spirit world. On the Northwest Coast, where the culture was preoccupied with class status, shamans were a class apart; they lived separately from their fellow tribespeople and passed their knowledge to their heirs.

Much of the healers' art consisted of ritual, but medicinal treatments were available, too. Sweathouses and steambaths were common throughout North America, and they were used for ritual purification before and after Vision Quests, battles, tribal ceremonies and other events, as well as for treating illnesses. Older people suffering from rheumatism and anyone nursing a cold or fever could find some relief in the warm steam. Herbs and plant potions were also prescribed, and many — such as willow and poplar, which contain the same compound as

ABOVE: Members of the Fool Dance Society of the Assiniboine and Gros Ventres tribes. The Fool Dance is one of the few dances of the northern Plains in which participants wear masks. This 1906 photo was taken by Sumner W. Matteson at Fort Belknap Reservation in Montana.

RIGHT: Most tribes had healers and shamans to look after their physical and spiritual welfare. Here, in a photo taken by Edward S. Curtis, a Kwakiutl Twin Child Healer ministers to a patient. Eagle feathers and sharp sticks thrust through baskets were believed to have curative powers.

BELOW: A member of the Hamatsa Dance Society of the Kwakiutl tribe, photographed by Curtis.

aspirin — have been vindicated by contemporary medicine. Healers also cleaned wounds, poulticed boils, manipulated dislocated bones back into position and splinted broken ones. These curatives might seem mild, but many of the more serious diseases that are part of our lives today were not at all common in North America a few hundred years ago. Heart disease and cancer were rare and so were most viral and bacterial diseases; that's why, when the Europeans brought new strains of illness to the continent, whole tribes were virtually wiped out and others dramatically reduced in size.

Some conditions were believed to have supernatural origins that had to be treated by spiritual means. If it was determined that a malevolent spirit had found its way into the body, shamans had various ministrations for getting it out. Rituals that involved blowing, sucking and fanning out the sickness with feathers were all performed. Whistles, drums and healing rattles made of gourds, animal hooves or turtle shells were common. In California, shamans carried bundles of healing tokens. These were passed down from elder shaman tutors or by healing societies, and were likely to contain herbs, grinding tools, obsidian knives, ceremonial paint and rattles. In the Arctic, shamans wore knots tied under their clothing.

Some illnesses were believed to require direct contact with the spirit world. On the

Northwest Coast, shamans went into trances in which their souls were thought to cross over to the spirit world. There, a shaman might buy back the sick person's soul. Inuit shamans made similar journeys when ministering to the sick, except that theirs were believed to be underwater journeys. Once in the spirit world, shamans tried to recover the souls of their patients before they entered the realm of the dead. If the shamans were successful, they used ivory containers called soul catchers to hold the recovered souls. Sometimes they returned empty-handed; if the soul had eaten in the realm of the dead, it could not return to the human world. Based on their intimate knowledge of the supernatural, Arctic shamans also directed the carving of driftwood masks that were used during community ceremonies and dances. Men wore these large masks, while women wore finger-mask versions and danced behind the men.

In some tribes, the healer and the shaman were one and the same. In others, there were two separate occupations. In the Arctic, shamans handled the spiritual ills, but left physical cures to women healers who tended the sick with leeches, herbs, amulets and songs. Among the Navajo and Apache, the shaman would go into a trance to make a diagnosis and prescribe a ritual treatment; then masked healers took over, creating sacred sand paintings as altars over which to perform sacred chants. These ritual treatments could take as long as nine days. At the end of the ceremony, masked performers depicting Yeis, important Navajo spirits, came before the people to teach them about the spirit world. When they finished their performance, they removed their masks to show the continuity between the spirit and human worlds.

In the Northeast Woodlands, healing societies tended the sick. One such group was the False Face Society. Its members wore masks cut from living trees and carved to represent the faces of the spirits. Those who were cured were obliged to join the society. Another Northeast Woodlands group was the Husk Face Society, whose members wore corn husk masks.

Among the Algonquins, the Midewiwan, or Grand Medicine Society, met yearly to perform ceremonies for healing and conjuring. The Grand Medicine Dance was a frenzied ceremony in which the dancers used shells thought to have curative powers.

LEFT: A Pueblo dance kilt of tanned buffalo hide trimmed with tin cones and painted designs. The mid-19th century kilt bears the image of a snake, which was considered a sacred messenger to the spirit world.

BELOW LEFT: A collection of Hopi Kachina dolls, circa 1900-1920, representing various spirits.

Bibliography

Cox, Beverly and Martin Jacobs, *The Spirit of the Harvest: North American Indian Cooking*. New York: Stewart, Tabori & Chang, 1991.

Bancroft-Hunt, Norman, *North American Indians*. Philadelphia: Running Press, 1992.

Brafford, C.J. and Laine Thom, eds. *Dancing Colors: Paths of Native American Women*. San Francisco: Chronicle Books, 1992.

Campbell, David, ed. *Native American Art and Folklore: A Cultural Celebration*. Greenwich, CT: Brompton Books, 1993.

Champagne, Duane, ed. *Chronology of Native American History from Pre-Columbian Times to the Present*. Detroit: Gale Research, Inc., 1994.

Damas, David, ed. *Handbook of North American Indians, Volume 5: Arctic*. Washington, D.C.: Smithsonian Institution, 1984.

Goodchild, Peter, *Survival Skills of the North American Indians*. Chicago: Chicago Review Press, 1984.

Harrison, Lynn, *Traditions: Beadwork of the Native American*. Spokane, WA: Cheney Cowles Museum, Eastern Washington State Historical Society, 1990.

Hultkranz, Ake, *Native Religions of North America*. San Francisco: Harper & Row, 1987.

Kopper, Philip, *The Smithsonian Book of North American Indians Before the Coming of the Europeans*. Washington, D.C.: Smithsonian Books, 1986.

McCoy, Ronald, "Circles of Power," *Plateau*, The Museum of Northern Arizona, Vol. 55, No. 4, 1988.

Miles, Charles, *Indian and Eskimo Artifacts of North America*. New York: American Legacy Press, 1963.

Tedlock, Dennis, and Barbara Tedlock, eds. *Teachings from the American Earth*. New York: Liveright, 1975.

Thom, Laine, ed. *Becoming Brave: The Path to Native American Manhood*. San Francisco: Chronicle Books,1992.

Turner, Geoffrey, *Indians of North America*. New York: Sterling Publishing Co., Inc., 1979.

Walters, Anna Lee, *The Spirit of Native America: Beauty and Mysticism in American Indian Art*. San Francisco: Chronicle Books, 1989.

Yenne, Bill, *The Encyclopedia of North American Indian Tribes*. Greenwich, CT: Brompton Books, 1986.

Yenne, Bill, and Susan Garrett, *North American Indians*. Greenwich, CT: Brompton Books, 1984.

Acknowledgments

Special thanks go to Gregory W. Frazier, Ph.D., an American Indian activist, author and enrolled member of the Crow tribe who served as technical advisor; Beth Crowell, whose inspired design melded word and image so gracefully; Jean Martin, editor, whose expertise and encouragement were a joy; Rita Longabucco, whose energetic photo editing made the book come alive; Elizabeth Miles Montgomery, who prepared the index; Geraldine Ficarra, for her valuable insight; and my dear friend, Oscar, and my wonderful sister Ellen, for their support during this project.

Index

The geographic region of each tribe is identified by initials:

A – Arctic
SA – Sub-Arctic
NE – Northeast Woodlands
SE – Southeast
PP – Great Plains and Prairies
GB – Great Basin
SW – Southwest
C – California
NW – Northwest Coast

Page numbers in italics indicate illustrations.